EMMANUEL JOSEPH

Echoes of Innovation: The Heartbeats of Global Tech Hubs

Copyright © 2025 by Emmanuel Joseph

All rights reserved. No part of this publication may be reproduced, stored or transmitted in any form or by any means, electronic, mechanical, photocopying, recording, scanning, or otherwise without written permission from the publisher. It is illegal to copy this book, post it to a website, or distribute it by any other means without permission.

First edition

This book was professionally typeset on Reedsy.
Find out more at reedsy.com

Contents

1. Chapter 1: Introduction - The Global Tech Landscape — 1
2. Chapter 2: Silicon Valley - The Pioneer — 3
3. Chapter 3: Shenzhen - The Hardware Haven — 5
4. Chapter 4: Tel Aviv - The Startup Nation — 7
5. Chapter 5: Bangalore - The Silicon Plateau — 9
6. Chapter 6: Berlin - The Creative Tech Hub — 11
7. Chapter 7: Nairobi - The Silicon Savannah — 13
8. Chapter 8: Toronto - The Northern Beacon — 15
9. Chapter 9: Stockholm - The Unicorn Factory — 17
10. Chapter 10: Seoul - The Digital Dynamo — 19
11. Chapter 11: London - The Fintech Capital — 21
12. Chapter 12: Conclusion - The Future of Global Tech Hubs — 23

1

Chapter 1: Introduction - The Global Tech Landscape

In today's rapidly advancing world, technology serves as the bedrock of innovation, driving progress in myriad fields. From healthcare to finance, tech hubs around the globe serve as the lifeblood of our digital economy. These epicenters of creativity and ingenuity have transformed how we live, work, and communicate. Each tech hub has its unique story, shaped by cultural, economic, and political factors. This book delves into the heartbeats of these global tech hubs, exploring their histories, achievements, and challenges.

As we embark on this journey, it's essential to understand the pivotal role these hubs play. Not only do they foster groundbreaking technologies, but they also create jobs and fuel economic growth. They attract the brightest minds, driving innovation forward at an unprecedented pace. The competition among these hubs spurs advancements that ripple across the globe, impacting millions.

One of the most significant aspects of tech hubs is their ability to foster collaboration. The synergy between startups, established companies, academia, and governments creates an ecosystem where ideas flourish. This interconnectedness is vital for addressing complex global challenges, from climate change to healthcare. The exchange of knowledge and expertise propels innovation beyond geographical boundaries.

However, tech hubs also face unique challenges. The rapid pace of technological change can lead to ethical dilemmas and societal disruptions. Issues such as data privacy, cybersecurity, and the digital divide must be addressed to ensure that technological advancements benefit all. As we explore each tech hub, we'll consider how they navigate these challenges.

Understanding the historical context of these hubs is crucial. Many began as centers of industry or commerce before transforming into tech powerhouses. Their evolution reflects broader economic and social trends, offering insights into the factors that drive innovation. By examining their journeys, we can glean lessons for fostering innovation in other regions.

Finally, this book aims to celebrate the diversity of innovation across the globe. From Silicon Valley's entrepreneurial spirit to Shenzhen's manufacturing prowess, each hub has its strengths. Together, they form a vibrant tapestry of creativity and progress, echoing the heartbeat of global innovation.

2

Chapter 2: Silicon Valley - The Pioneer

Silicon Valley, nestled in California's Bay Area, stands as the quintessential tech hub. Its transformation from an agricultural region to the epicenter of technological innovation is a testament to the power of entrepreneurship. The seeds of Silicon Valley's success were sown in the mid-20th century, with the establishment of institutions like Stanford University and pioneering companies like Hewlett-Packard.

The region's unique blend of academia, venture capital, and a risk-taking culture has fueled its rise. Iconic companies such as Apple, Google, and Facebook have their roots here, shaping the digital landscape. The entrepreneurial spirit that pervades Silicon Valley encourages experimentation and drives continuous innovation.

However, success has brought challenges. The high cost of living and housing shortages have made it difficult for many to afford to live and work in the area. Additionally, issues of diversity and inclusion have come to the forefront, prompting calls for more equitable opportunities. Despite these challenges, Silicon Valley remains a beacon of innovation.

One of the key drivers of Silicon Valley's success is its robust startup ecosystem. The availability of venture capital and a supportive network of mentors and advisors create an environment conducive to new ventures. Startups thrive on the region's culture of collaboration and its willingness to embrace failure as a stepping stone to success.

The role of universities and research institutions cannot be overstated. Stanford University, in particular, has been instrumental in fostering innovation. Its strong ties with industry and emphasis on entrepreneurship have produced generations of innovators who continue to shape the tech world. The interplay between academia and industry is a hallmark of Silicon Valley's ecosystem.

Looking to the future, Silicon Valley faces both opportunities and challenges. The region's ability to adapt to changing technological trends and address societal issues will determine its continued relevance. As we explore other tech hubs, we'll see how they draw inspiration from Silicon Valley's successes and lessons.

3

Chapter 3: Shenzhen - The Hardware Haven

Shenzhen, once a modest fishing village in southern China, has undergone a dramatic transformation. Today, it stands as a global hub for hardware innovation and manufacturing. The city's rise to prominence began in the late 20th century, driven by government policies and investments in infrastructure. Shenzhen's strategic location near Hong Kong also played a crucial role in its development.

One of the defining features of Shenzhen is its manufacturing prowess. The city is home to a vast network of factories and suppliers, making it a hotspot for hardware startups. Companies like Huawei and DJI have leveraged this ecosystem to become global leaders in their respective fields. The concept of "Shanzhai" or copycat products, once prevalent, has evolved into a culture of rapid innovation and iteration.

Shenzhen's success is also attributed to its favorable business environment. Government policies, such as tax incentives and streamlined regulations, have attracted both domestic and international entrepreneurs. The city's commitment to fostering innovation is evident in its numerous tech parks and incubators that support startups from inception to scale.

However, Shenzhen faces challenges as it strives to maintain its competitive edge. Intellectual property issues and international scrutiny have raised concerns about the sustainability of its growth. Additionally, the city must navigate the complexities of balancing rapid urbanization with environmental sustainability. Addressing these challenges will be crucial for Shenzhen's long-term success.

The role of collaboration in Shenzhen's ecosystem cannot be overstated. The city's open and cooperative culture has fostered partnerships between startups, established companies, and research institutions. This synergy drives continuous innovation and ensures that Shenzhen remains at the forefront of hardware development. The city's commitment to research and development is also reflected in its significant investments in cutting-edge technologies.

Looking ahead, Shenzhen's influence on global tech innovation is poised to grow. The city's ability to adapt to emerging trends and address challenges will determine its continued success. As we explore other tech hubs, we'll see how Shenzhen's model of rapid iteration and collaboration inspires innovation worldwide.

4

Chapter 4: Tel Aviv - The Startup Nation

Tel Aviv, Israel's vibrant coastal city, has earned the moniker "Startup Nation" due to its prolific startup ecosystem. Despite its small size and limited natural resources, Israel has become a global leader in technology and innovation. Tel Aviv, in particular, has played a pivotal role in this transformation, driven by a unique combination of factors.

One of the key drivers of Tel Aviv's success is its strong entrepreneurial culture. The city boasts a high concentration of startups per capita, with innovators pushing the boundaries of technology in fields such as cybersecurity, artificial intelligence, and biotech. Notable companies like Waze and Mobileye have their origins in Tel Aviv, showcasing the city's global impact.

Military technology has also played a significant role in Tel Aviv's tech landscape. Many entrepreneurs and engineers gain valuable experience during their mandatory military service, particularly in elite units focused on technology and intelligence. This experience often translates into innovative solutions for civilian applications, driving the city's tech ecosystem forward.

However, Tel Aviv faces challenges as it continues to grow as a tech hub. Geopolitical tensions in the region can impact business operations and investment. Additionally, the city's high cost of living poses challenges for both residents and startups. Addressing these issues will be crucial for Tel Aviv's sustained success.

The role of government and public policy is also significant in Tel Aviv's tech ecosystem. The Israeli government has implemented various initiatives to support startups, including funding programs, tax incentives, and support for research and development. These efforts have created a conducive environment for innovation and entrepreneurship.

Looking ahead, Tel Aviv's influence on global tech innovation is set to expand. The city's ability to adapt to emerging trends and address challenges will determine its continued relevance. As we explore other tech hubs, we'll see how Tel Aviv's unique blend of military technology, entrepreneurial spirit, and government support drives innovation.

5

Chapter 5: Bangalore - The Silicon Plateau

Bangalore, often referred to as the Silicon Valley of India, has emerged as a major global tech hub. The city's journey from an outsourcing center to a hub of innovation and entrepreneurship is a testament to its resilience and adaptability. Bangalore's rise has been driven by a combination of factors, including a strong talent pool, favorable policies, and a thriving startup ecosystem.

The city's tech landscape is dominated by major companies such as Infosys, Wipro, and Flipkart. These companies have played a crucial role in shaping Bangalore's tech ecosystem, attracting talent, and fostering innovation. The presence of multinational corporations and research institutions further enhances the city's appeal as a tech hub.

Bangalore's entrepreneurial spirit is evident in its vibrant startup scene. The city is home to numerous startups working on cutting-edge technologies in fields such as fintech, edtech, and healthtech. The availability of venture capital and support from incubators and accelerators has created an environment conducive to innovation and risk-taking.

However, Bangalore faces challenges as it continues to grow as a tech hub. Infrastructure issues, such as traffic congestion and inadequate public transportation, pose significant challenges. Additionally, the city must address concerns related to brain drain and market competition. Ensuring sustainable growth will be crucial for Bangalore's long-term success.

The role of government and public policy in Bangalore's tech ecosystem is also significant. The Indian government has implemented various initiatives to support startups and foster innovation, including funding programs, tax incentives, and support for research and development. These efforts have created a conducive environment for growth and entrepreneurship.

Looking ahead, Bangalore's influence on global tech innovation is set to expand. The city's ability to adapt to emerging trends and address challenges will determine its continued relevance. As we explore other tech hubs, we'll see how Bangalore's unique blend of talent, entrepreneurial spirit, and government support drives innovation.

6

Chapter 6: Berlin - The Creative Tech Hub

Berlin, Germany's capital, has emerged as a vibrant tech hub characterized by its unique blend of creativity and technology. The city's transformation from a divided post-war city to a flourishing center of innovation is a remarkable story. Berlin's rich cultural history and diverse population contribute to its dynamic tech scene, making it an attractive destination for entrepreneurs and creatives alike.

The city's startup ecosystem is thriving, with a focus on sectors such as fintech, e-commerce, and mobility. Notable companies like Zalando, N26, and Delivery Hero have their roots in Berlin, showcasing the city's potential to produce global tech leaders. The presence of coworking spaces, incubators, and accelerators further supports the growth of startups, fostering collaboration and innovation.

Government support plays a significant role in Berlin's tech ecosystem. The German government and the European Union have implemented various initiatives to encourage entrepreneurship and innovation, including funding programs, tax incentives, and support for research and development. These efforts create a conducive environment for startups to flourish and scale.

However, Berlin faces challenges as it continues to grow as a tech hub. Competition from other European cities, such as London and Amsterdam, poses a constant challenge. Additionally, securing adequate funding for startups can be difficult, especially for early-stage ventures. Addressing these challenges is crucial for Berlin's sustained success in the tech landscape.

Berlin's creative culture sets it apart from other tech hubs. The city's vibrant arts scene, coupled with its emphasis on collaboration and diversity, fosters a unique environment where innovation thrives. This creative energy is reflected in the city's tech companies, which often incorporate design and user experience into their products and services.

Looking ahead, Berlin's influence on the European tech ecosystem is poised to grow. The city's ability to attract talent, foster collaboration, and navigate challenges will determine its continued relevance. As we explore other tech hubs, we'll see how Berlin's unique blend of creativity and technology drives innovation in the region.

7

Chapter 7: Nairobi - The Silicon Savannah

Nairobi, the capital of Kenya, has emerged as a leading tech hub in Africa, often referred to as the "Silicon Savannah." The city's rise to prominence is a testament to its entrepreneurial spirit and innovative solutions to local challenges. Nairobi's tech landscape is characterized by a focus on mobile technology, fintech, and social impact ventures.

One of the most significant innovations to come out of Nairobi is M-Pesa, a mobile banking platform that has revolutionized financial inclusion in Kenya and beyond. The success of M-Pesa has spurred the growth of other fintech startups, positioning Nairobi as a leader in mobile financial services. This innovation has had a profound impact on the lives of millions, providing access to financial services for the unbanked.

Government and international support play a crucial role in Nairobi's tech ecosystem. Various initiatives and partnerships have been established to support startups and foster innovation. These efforts include funding programs, capacity-building initiatives, and infrastructure development, creating an environment conducive to entrepreneurship.

However, Nairobi faces challenges as it continues to grow as a tech hub. Infrastructure issues, such as unreliable electricity and limited internet connectivity, pose significant obstacles. Additionally, securing adequate funding for startups can be challenging, particularly for early-stage ventures.

Addressing these issues is crucial for Nairobi's sustained growth and success.

Nairobi's tech scene is also characterized by its focus on social impact. Many startups in the city aim to address pressing local issues, such as access to healthcare, education, and clean energy. This focus on social innovation not only drives economic growth but also contributes to the well-being of the community.

Looking ahead, Nairobi's influence on the African tech ecosystem is set to expand. The city's ability to adapt to emerging trends, foster collaboration, and address challenges will determine its continued relevance. As we explore other tech hubs, we'll see how Nairobi's unique blend of innovation and social impact drives progress in the region.

8

Chapter 8: Toronto - The Northern Beacon

Toronto, Canada's largest city, has emerged as a major tech hub in North America. The city's rise to prominence is driven by its diverse talent pool, robust academic institutions, and supportive government policies. Toronto's tech landscape is characterized by a focus on artificial intelligence, fintech, and enterprise software.

One of the key drivers of Toronto's success is its strong talent pool. The city's universities, such as the University of Toronto and Ryerson University, produce a steady stream of skilled graduates in fields like computer science and engineering. This talent, combined with immigration policies that attract skilled workers from around the world, creates a vibrant and diverse workforce.

Toronto's tech ecosystem is home to major players such as Shopify and Blackberry, as well as numerous startups and emerging ventures. The city's entrepreneurial spirit is supported by a network of incubators, accelerators, and venture capital firms, creating an environment conducive to innovation and growth.

Government support plays a significant role in Toronto's tech ecosystem. The Canadian government has implemented various initiatives to encourage entrepreneurship and innovation, including funding programs, tax incentives, and support for research and development. These efforts create a conducive environment for startups to flourish and scale.

However, Toronto faces challenges as it continues to grow as a tech hub. Competition from other North American cities, such as Silicon Valley and New York, poses a constant challenge. Additionally, securing adequate funding for startups can be difficult, particularly for early-stage ventures. Addressing these challenges is crucial for Toronto's sustained success in the tech landscape.

Looking ahead, Toronto's influence on the global tech ecosystem is poised to grow. The city's ability to attract talent, foster collaboration, and navigate challenges will determine its continued relevance. As we explore other tech hubs, we'll see how Toronto's unique blend of talent, entrepreneurial spirit, and government support drives innovation.

9

Chapter 9: Stockholm - The Unicorn Factory

Stockholm, the capital of Sweden, has earned the nickname "The Unicorn Factory" due to its impressive track record of producing billion-dollar companies. The city's rise as a tech hub is driven by its strong innovation culture, supportive government policies, and a focus on sustainability. Stockholm's tech landscape is characterized by a thriving startup ecosystem and notable success stories.

One of the key drivers of Stockholm's success is its historical legacy of innovation. Sweden has a long history of pioneering inventions and technological advancements, from the Nobel Prize to the pacemaker. This legacy has fostered a culture of innovation that continues to thrive in Stockholm's tech scene.

Stockholm is home to notable startups and tech giants, such as Spotify, Skype, and Klarna. These companies have not only achieved global success but also inspired a new generation of entrepreneurs. The presence of coworking spaces, incubators, and accelerators further supports the growth of startups, fostering collaboration and innovation.

Government support plays a significant role in Stockholm's tech ecosystem. The Swedish government has implemented various initiatives to encourage entrepreneurship and innovation, including funding programs, tax incentives, and support for research and development. These efforts create a conducive environment for startups to flourish and scale.

However, Stockholm faces challenges as it continues to grow as a tech hub. Market competition and scaling internationally can pose significant obstacles. Additionally, securing adequate funding for startups can be challenging, particularly for early-stage ventures. Addressing these challenges is crucial for Stockholm's sustained success in the tech landscape.

Looking ahead, Stockholm's influence on the global tech ecosystem is set to expand. The city's ability to attract talent, foster collaboration, and navigate challenges will determine its continued relevance. As we explore other tech hubs, we'll see how Stockholm's unique blend of innovation, sustainability, and government support drives progress.

10

Chapter 10: Seoul - The Digital Dynamo

Seoul, the capital of South Korea, has emerged as a digital powerhouse in Asia. The city's rapid technological advancement post-Korean War is a testament to its resilience and innovation. Seoul's tech landscape is characterized by a focus on consumer electronics, telecommunications, and smart city solutions.

One of the key drivers of Seoul's success is its emphasis on research and development. South Korea invests heavily in R&D, with a significant portion of its GDP dedicated to innovation. This investment has propelled companies like Samsung and LG to the forefront of the global tech industry, showcasing Seoul's potential as a tech hub.

Seoul's tech ecosystem is also characterized by its strong government support. The South Korean government has implemented various initiatives to encourage entrepreneurship and innovation, including funding programs, tax incentives, and support for research and development. These efforts create a conducive environment for startups to flourish and scale.

However, Seoul faces challenges as it continues to grow as a tech hub. Geopolitical tensions in the region can impact business operations and investment. Additionally, the city must address concerns related to market competition and scaling internationally. Ensuring sustainable growth will be crucial for Seoul's long-term success.

Seoul's tech scene is also characterized by its focus on smart city solutions.

The city has implemented various initiatives to improve urban living through technology, such as smart transportation systems and energy-efficient buildings. This focus on smart city solutions not only drives economic growth but also contributes to the well-being of residents.

Looking ahead, Seoul's influence on the global tech ecosystem is poised to grow. The city's ability to adapt to emerging trends, foster collaboration, and address challenges will determine its continued relevance. As we explore other tech hubs, we'll see how Seoul's unique blend of research and development, government support, and smart city initiatives drives innovation.

11

Chapter 11: London - The Fintech Capital

London, the capital of the United Kingdom, has emerged as a global tech and fintech hub. The city's evolution from a financial center to a tech powerhouse is driven by its diverse talent pool, robust academic institutions, and supportive government policies. London's tech landscape is characterized by a focus on financial technology, cybersecurity, and artificial intelligence.

One of the key drivers of London's success is its strong financial services sector. The city's status as a global financial center has created a natural synergy with fintech innovation. Notable companies like Revolut, TransferWise, and Monzo have their roots in London, showcasing the city's potential to produce global tech leaders.

London's tech ecosystem is supported by a network of accelerators, incubators, and coworking spaces that foster collaboration and innovation. The presence of world-class universities, such as Imperial College London and University College London, further enhances the city's appeal as a tech hub. These institutions produce a steady stream of skilled graduates who contribute to the city's vibrant tech scene.

Government support plays a significant role in London's tech ecosystem. Various initiatives, such as the UK government's fintech strategy and support for research and development, create a conducive environment for startups and established companies alike. These efforts have positioned London as a leading destination for tech investment and innovation.

However, London faces challenges as it continues to grow as a tech hub. The uncertainties surrounding Brexit have raised concerns about access to talent and investment. Additionally, competition from other global tech hubs, such as New York and Singapore, poses a constant challenge. Addressing these issues is crucial for London's sustained success in the tech landscape.

Looking ahead, London's influence on the global tech and fintech ecosystems is poised to grow. The city's ability to attract talent, foster collaboration, and navigate challenges will determine its continued relevance. As we explore other tech hubs, we'll see how London's unique blend of financial services expertise, entrepreneurial spirit, and government support drives innovation.

12

Chapter 12: Conclusion - The Future of Global Tech Hubs

As we conclude our journey through the world's leading tech hubs, it's clear that innovation knows no boundaries. From Silicon Valley to Shenzhen, each hub has its unique strengths and challenges, contributing to a diverse and interconnected global tech ecosystem. The stories of these tech hubs highlight the importance of collaboration, resilience, and adaptability in driving progress.

The future of global tech hubs will be shaped by emerging technologies and trends. Fields such as artificial intelligence, blockchain, and biotechnology are poised to revolutionize industries and create new opportunities for innovation. Tech hubs that can harness these technologies and foster a culture of continuous learning will lead the way in the next wave of innovation.

International collaboration and knowledge exchange will play a crucial role in addressing global challenges. Tech hubs must work together to solve pressing issues such as climate change, healthcare, and inequality. By leveraging their collective expertise, these hubs can drive meaningful change and create a more inclusive and sustainable future.

However, the rapid pace of technological change also presents ethical dilemmas and societal disruptions. Issues such as data privacy, cybersecurity, and the digital divide must be addressed to ensure that technological advancements benefit all. Tech hubs must navigate these challenges thoughtfully, prioritizing the well-being of society and the environment.

The importance of fostering inclusive and equitable innovation cannot be overstated. Tech hubs must strive to create opportunities for diverse voices and perspectives, ensuring that everyone can participate in and benefit from technological progress. By embracing diversity, these hubs can drive more creative and impactful solutions to global challenges.

In conclusion, the heartbeats of global tech hubs echo with the promise of innovation and progress. As we look to the future, it's clear that these hubs will continue to play a pivotal role in shaping our world. By fostering collaboration, resilience, and inclusivity, they can drive meaningful change and create a brighter future for all. The journey of innovation is far from over, and the best is yet to come.

Echoes of Innovation: The Heartbeats of Global Tech Hubs

Echoes of Innovation: The Heartbeats of Global Tech Hubs is a captivating journey through the world's leading centers of technology and innovation. This book delves deep into the unique stories of tech hubs across the globe, exploring their histories, achievements, and challenges. From the pioneering spirit of Silicon Valley to the rapid iteration and manufacturing prowess of Shenzhen, each chapter highlights the distinctive qualities that make these hubs pulse with creativity and progress.

Readers will discover how Tel Aviv, known as the Startup Nation, leverages military technology for civilian innovation, and how Nairobi's groundbreaking mobile banking solutions have transformed financial inclusion. The vibrant startup culture of Berlin, the sustainability-focused unicorn factory of Stockholm, and the entrepreneurial spirit of Bangalore are just a few of the diverse ecosystems featured in this book.

Echoes of Innovation also examines the critical role of government policies, the importance of fostering collaboration, and the unique challenges each tech hub faces. Through this exploration, readers gain insights into how these innovation centers address issues such as data privacy, cybersecurity, and the digital divide. The book celebrates the diversity of global tech hubs and offers a vision for a more inclusive and sustainable future.

CHAPTER 12: CONCLUSION - THE FUTURE OF GLOBAL TECH HUBS

With engaging narratives and a thorough analysis of each tech hub's evolution, this book provides a comprehensive understanding of the dynamic forces driving technological progress worldwide. Whether you're a tech enthusiast, entrepreneur, or curious reader, **Echoes of Innovation** promises to inspire and enlighten, showcasing the vibrant tapestry of creativity that shapes our digital world.

www.ingramcontent.com/pod-product-compliance
Lightning Source LLC
LaVergne TN
LVHW020743090526
838202LV00057BA/6207